First published in Great Britain 2015 by Rethink Press (www.rethinkpress.com)

Illustration and book design by Victrixia Montes

eMpower Yourself
with 7 Natural Laws

WIIFY – What's In It For You?

Are you a thinker? It is said that most people are engaged in mental activities and they call it thinking. That is not thinking…! When you start thinking of the possibilities of what you can be, do and have; now that take's some real thinking.

It requires real conscious effort to believe in yourself and to shape your life the way you really want it.

Live By This Absolute Truth...

There is a thinking stuff from which all things are made, and which, in its original state, permeates, penetrates, and fills the interspaces of the universe.

A thought in this substance produces the thing that is imaged by the thought.

A person can form things in his thought, and by impressing his thought upon formless substance, can cause the thing he thinks about to be created.

The Science of Getting Rich by Wallace D Wattles

eMpower Yourself with 7 Natural Laws is designed to assist you in your thinking process by offering you immediate help by way of great quotes, questions, poems, short stories and wise words that really can shape your mood both personally and professionally.

You see the ordinary people, who achieve great things, are people who are in control of their thinking. They think what they want and hang onto it until they accomplish it. It's not what happens to you that matters, but rather, what you think and do about what happens that really matters... in order words, how you react to what happens to you.

People who refuse to let circumstances or other people dictate, their daily mood are people who:

- Stay calm in the midst of the storm and enjoy life
- Never take their eyes off what is truly important (the job at hand)
- Make dreams come true (the goal achievers of this world)

eMpower Yourself with 7 Natural Laws is essentially for you in those moments, when you feel like, "You're losing it" or "You can't cope" because, that is the time to seek assistance or help. Sometimes all you need is a few encouraging words or a reminder about how to cope or perhaps a change of focus through asking yourself the right quality question. Sometimes it is humor that breaks your pattern, from one of depression or sadness, or simply an opportunity to laugh at one's predicament or self.

eMpower Yourself with 7 Natural Laws is a collection of quotes, questions, poems, short stories and wise words. These quotes, questions, poems, short stories and wise words have been passed down through the generations at times when help has been most required. They are words of wisdom that remind us to keep our thoughts – Pure, Positive, Purposeful, Productive and People-Focused.

Keep it in your draw or on your desk at work or on your coffee table or on your bedside table or anywhere, you can easily access the book. Refer to it daily and randomly select the mood you choose to be in, in the moment by the corresponding colour to reveal your personal message.

Meet
the author: Tosin Ogunnusi
(The UK's No. 1 Empowerment Activities Trainer)

Originally from Lagos, Nigeria, Oluwatosin Ogunnusi, is a Professional Fire-walking, Board Breaking, Bar Bending, Arrow Breaking and Glass-walking Instructor & Trainer, Hypnotherapist, Trainer of NeuroLinguistic Programming (NLP). Certified and registered with, The American Board of NLP (ABNLP), since 2006.

"Tosin," as he is known by his friends, family and colleagues, has trained thousands of people worldwide, and is a very dynamic and charismatic presenter.

Art and design by **Victrixia Montes**

Tosin now heads up Mpowerment Ltd.'s Motivational Training for corporate clients along with running its flagship events, **"1 Day Team-building Empowerment Day"**, **"4 Days Empowerment Activities Instructor Training"** (EAIT) and "3 Days Speaking & Presenting with IMPACT Program" (SPWI).

Tosin's experience and passion lies in helping individuals and organizations improve their performance, with over 12+ years experience in Personal Development, Sales and Leadership within a range of organizations. His company has worked with the likes of the **FA** (Football Association in the UK), **Aviva** (One of the largest insurance companies in the UK) and **o2** (The Telephone company)…Just to mention a few…!

The idea to produce "**eMpower Yourself** with 7 Natural Laws" came from Tosin's desire to ignite his own passion and others on a daily basis. He wanted to have something to fuel himself everyday, when he woke up in the morning, during lunch at work and when he got home at night just before going to bed.

He loved the idea of having all his favourite sayings, quotes, questions, poems, short stories and wise words readily available in one place for inspiration and motivation.

He cleverly links the sayings, quotes, questions, poems, short stories and wise words to the, **"Rainbow Colours, (Red, Orange, Yellow, Green, Blue, Indigo and Purple)."**

Colours are great for shaping our moods. Depending on how we are feeling in any given moment, certain colours will resonate better than others – And colours also have the power to heal our souls. He hopes you derive as much inspiration and motivation from them just as he has. **Happy, Wealthy and Healthy Living!**

Love More, Laugh Often and Live Well…!

The Colour Key:

Red

The colour red is the colour of energy, passion & action. Red is a physical colour, which calls for action to be taken. Its high energy and strength draws attention to itself and demands to be noticed.

Key words are: Energy, Action, Desire, Passion, Assertive, Powerful, Exciting, Confident, Courageous, Strong, Spontaneous, Determined, Driven and Stimulating.

Orange

The colour orange is the colour of adventure and social communication. Orange is a colour of adventure, which inspires and creates enthusiasm. It is optimistic and sociable and suggests affordability.

Key words: Adventure, Risk Taking, Uninhibited, Independent, Flamboyant, Extroverted, Creative Flair, Warm-Hearted, Agreeable & Informal, Friendship, Social Communication & Interaction, Courage, Enthusiasm, Rejuvenation

Yellow

The colour yellow is the colour of the mind and the intellect. Yellow is an illuminating and uplifting colour, which stimulates our analytical processes and assists with mental clarity.

Key words: Mind & Intellect, Optimistic & Cheerful, Academic, Analytical, Wisdom, Logic, Enthusiasm, Fun, Good-Humoured, Challenging, Originality, Creativity, Cheerfulness, Optimism and Confidence

Green

The colour green is the colour of balance, harmony and growth. Green is associated with nature, health and healing. It balances the emotions and inspires compassion.

Key words: Rejuvenating, Nurturing, Dependable, Balance & Growth, Hope, Self-Reliance, Agreeable and Diplomatic, Nature Lover, Family Oriented, Practical & Down to earth, Calm & Kind, Generous, Sympathetic, Compassionate, Emotionally Balanced, Harmony and Renewal & Restoration.

Blue

The colour blue is the colour of trust and responsibility. Blue is the safest colour to use in most applications, implying honesty, trust and dependability.

Key words: Peace & Calm, Honesty, Authority, Religion, Wisdom, Trust & Peace, Loyalty & Integrity, Responsibility, Tactful, Reliability, Perseverance, Caring, Devotion, Orderly, Concern, Idealistic, Contemplation, Peaceful and Organized.

Indigo

The colour of intuition, perception and higher mind, Indigo is a powerful and strong colour, which conveys integrity & sincerity. It is associated with structure & rituals.

Key words: Intuition, Idealism, Structure & Order, Wisdom, Selflessness, Regulations, Highly Intuitive, Practical Visionary and Faithful

Purple

The colour purple is the colour of imagination and spirituality. Purple implies, wealth, quality, fantasy & creativity. It works well with many other colours.

Key words: Imagination, Unusual & Individual, Creative, Individuality, Spirituality, Inspiration, Psychic & Intuitive, Humanitarian, Creative & Inventive, Selfless & Unlimited, Mystery, Fantasy & Future.

The Origin (God), created you and your
planet for your complete enjoyment.

••

Live every day to the full,
as if it was your last.

••

Be Happy & Fun
Be Thoughtful & Respectful
Be Grateful & Appreciative
Be Proactive & Productive
Be Attentive & Peaceful
Be Kind & Reliable
Be Purposeful & Meaningful
Be Generous & Giving
Be Aware of Self & Others and thank God you are alive!

The Law of Perpetual Transmutation

All you are is ENERGY!

Energy moves into physical form and the images you hold in your mind...

...most often materialize in RESULTS in your LIFE.

So, create the right images for you today...

www.Mpowerment.co.uk

What is the most **IMPORTANT** *thing you have to get done today?*

PRODUCTIVITY

What do you have to accomplish today to progress you further up the ladder in terms of attaining your goal?

TOUGH TIMES
DON'T LAST

TOUGH
PEOPLE
DO

FLOYD MAYWEATHER JR

www.Mpowerment.co.uk

NOTHING is TERMINAL.

EVERYTHING is TRANSITIONAL

What looks like the EN
of the road will turn ou
to be a BEND…

Robert Schulle

The Winner's Creed

I am a fighter.
Every problem in life, every struggle, is merely a game for me to enjoy and win.
I am an intelligent fighter,
using the brain and instinct for survival that was passed on to me
by countless generations of ancestors, a genetic gift, my inheritance.
I am a winner, because I refuse to accept defeat:
I can only be defeated if I give up, which I never shall.
Every success makes me stronger.
Every experience makes me wiser.
Every new fight gives me another chance to win.
And I enjoy winning.
To the timid, the approaching battle looks worse than to the fighter.
It is magnified by fear, but reduced and overcome by courage.
I begin and finish a winner,
because I know that all I have to do is to stay strong and keep fighting,
until I tire out the opposition.
That is the rule of persistence and determination
- that the last man on his feet is the winner.
Merely being prepared and willing to fight is my greatest asset.
I shall always strive to be a winner.

www.Mpowerment.co.uk   ~ Unknown

I WILL WIN

The die has been cast, I've stepped over the line.

The decision has been done the destiny's been determined.

I will no longer vacillate. I will no longer vacate.

I will no longer listen to, listen at or listen in on losing.

I will not be defeated, dejected, diluted or detoured.

I will no longer navigate with the needle of negativity.

The direction's been decided, the trail to be tried.

The destiny directed the future forged.

I will not be pulled on, pulled in, pulled down or pulled out.

I won't back up, back down or back away or back off.

I won't give in, give out or even give way to defeat.

I no longer will meander in the maze of mediocrity.

I will no longer conform to the cancer of can't.

I now will confirm the condition of can.

I will, probe, the possibilities, pick the probabilities.

I will focus on the fire and heat it even hotter.

I will never give up, let up, set up or shut up on success.

I am reaching for the ring, pulling on the power.

I've quit wishing, hoping, wasting and whining.

I now will aggressively gear into the word go.
And I am determined to dare to do till I drop.
I will withstand the whining winds of defeat.
And I will be powerfully persistent, consistent and insistent.
To get out of life what I truly deserve Because I am willing,
I am waiting, I am worthy and I understand
the only defeat is from within.
I now know that beyond any shadow of the cloud of doubt,
There is no shadow, there is no cloud, and there is no doubt.

I WILL WIN!

Unknown

www.Mpowerment.co.uk

Ask
and you will receive,

seek
and you will find,

knock
and the door will
be opened to you!

- Jesus Christ -

OPPORTUNITIES
are usually disguised by
HARDWORK

so most people don't recognize them.

~Ann Landers~

www.Mpowerment.co.uk

The fruit you **eat** comes from **trees** planted by someone else. **You** have to plant **trees** for those **who** will **follow** you.

Ask yourself, "What am I contributing to the forthcoming generations?".

THE LAW OF POLARITY

Everything has an opposite:

Hot - Cold

Up - Down

Good - Bad

Left - Right

Negative - Positive

Heads - Tails

Ugly - Beautiful

On - Off

Rich - Poor

Sad - Happy

Constantly look for the good in people and situations.
People love compliments and the positive idea in your mind.
When you find it, tell the person.
It makes you feel good about yourself for doing so.
Remember, good ideas – good vibrations.

www.Mpowerment.co.uk

www.Mpowerment.co.uk

" Choose a job you love and you will never have to work a day in your life "

Confucius

One of the big differences between sad people and happy people is that...

Sad people become negative evidence collectors, dutifully looking for AWFUL things, people, events, to put into a mental folder labeled PROOF LIFE IS AWFUL."

Happy people are positive evidence collectors, constantly looking for AWESOME things, people, events, to put into a mental folder labeled PROOF LIFE IS AWESOME.

Because happy people collect AWESOME not AWFUL stuff, they notice and attract more AWESOME stuff, thereby filling up their mental folders with lots of happy evidence that LIFE IS INDEED AWESOME.

Karen Salmansohn

YOU ARE NOT DEFEATED UNTIL YOU START BLAMING SOMEBODY ELSE.

TAKE FULL RESPONSIBILITY FOR YOUR LIFE...

ESPECIALLY, IF IT WASN'T YOUR FAULT.

THIS WILL ALLOW YOU TO TAKE THE CREDIT FOR BEING THE PERSON WHO DID SOMETHING ABOUT IT.

www.Mpowerment.co.uk

www.Mpowerment.co.uk

DON'T LOOK FOR WHOM
TO BLAME FOR THE PROBLEM,
LOOK FOR THE SOLUTION
TO THE PROBLEM

"You are either ON the WAY or you're IN the WAY and you have to make up your mind which one!"

Craig Valentine

www.Mpowerment.co.uk

"People make people and people break people

but you still need people around you!"

"IF YOU'RE DOING SOMETHING THEN YOU'LL GET CRITICIZED. THE ONLY PEOPLE WHO ARE NOT CRITICIZED ARE THOSE WHO DO NOTHING!"

www.Mpowerment.co.uk

The Law of Relativity

Nothing is good or bad, big or small...
until you RELATE/COMPARE it to something in your life.

Practice relating/comparing your situation
to something much worse
and yours will always look, feel, sound, taste and smell good!

Portia Nelson was at a seminar and participants were asked to write their life story on one page. She wrote:

Chapter 1
I walked down a street there is a deep hole in the sidewalk, I did not see the hole, I fall into the hole it takes forever to crawl out.

Chapter 2
I walked down the same street there is a deep hole in the sidewalk, I see the hole, I fall in, I eventually crawl out the hole.

Chapter 3
I walked down the same street there is a deep hole in the sidewalk, even though I see the hole, I still fall into the hole.
My God it's a habit I get out easier this time.

Chapter 4
I walked down the same street, there is a deep hole in the sidewalk, I see the hole, I walk round the hole.

Chapter 5
I walked down a different street.

Unhappiness is the hunger to get
happiness is the hunger to give.

W.G. Jordan (1864 – 1928)

What are you adding today?

www.Mpowerment.co.uk
PURPOSE
How can I serve
(my family, team, friends, colleagues, students, customers etc.)
to the best of my abilities today?

The mind is like a parachute.
It doesn't function until it's open.
OPEN YOUR MIND TODAY!

www.Mpowerment.co.uk

Showing up,
Being me, Going for it,
In the Moment, Sillier than ever,
GETTING IT WRONG,
Stop being right, Accepting others,
Loving myself,
DANCING WILDLY, STEPPING BEYOND,
Amazed at myself, I can't believe it,
I'm Coming Alive!

ED SHEAR

THERE'S ALWAYS A WAY

YOU

GOAL

IF YOU ARE WILLING TO PAY THE PRICE
IN TIME ENERGY OR EFFORT.

ROBERT H. SCHULLER

No person
has ever gone blind
from looking at the
bright side of life.

So, always look on the bright side of your life!

The Law of Vibration

Everything vibrates,

nothing rests

and conscious awareness of vibration is called feeling.

Your thoughts control your paradigms and your vibrations.

When you are not feeling good,

become aware of what you are thinking,

then think of something pleasant.

Go to a tranquil and peaceful place in your mind.

Physiology

Take care of your

PHYSICAL, MENTAL and SPIRITUAL body TODAY

Do you have the energy to survive today?

Are you well rested and fully hydrated today?

Are you eating well and exercising today?

by eating well, drinking well (at least 2 liters of water), sleeping well and exercising well today!

the Invitation

It does not interest me what you do for a living. I want to know what you ache for, and if you dare to dream of meeting your heart's longing. It does not interest me more how old you are. I want to know if you will risk looking like a fool for love, for your dream, for the adventure of being alive. It does not interest me what planets are squaring your moon. I want to know if you have touched the centre of your own sorrow—if you have been opened by life's betrayals or have become shrivelled and closed from fear of further pain. I want to know if you can sit with pain, mine or your own, without moving to hide from it or fade it or fix it. I want to know if you can be with joy—mine or your own, if you can dance with wildness, and let the ecstasy fill you to the tips of your fingers and toes without cautioning us to be careful—be realistic—to remember the limitation of being human. It does not interest me if the story you are telling is true I want to know if you can disappoint another to be true to yourself; if you can bear the accusation of betrayal and not betray your own soul; if you can be faithless and therefore trustworthy.

I want to know if you can see beauty even when it is not pretty everyday, and if you can source your own life from its presence. I want to know if you can live with failure—yours and mine—and still stand on the edge of the lake and shout to the silver of the full moon, "Yes!" It does not interest me to know how much money you have. I want to know if you can get up after the night of grief and despair, weary and bruised to the bone and do what needs to be done to feed the children. It does not interest me, who you know, or how you came to be here. I want to know if you will stand in the centre of the fire with me and not shrink back. It does not interest me where or what or with whom you have studied. I want to know what sustains you from the inside when all else falls away. I want to know if you can be alone with yourself and if you truly like the company you keep in the empty moments.

Oriah MountainDreamer

1994

The Rose

One day I was offered a beautiful Rose, which had a wonderful fragrance. I said to the Rose, The Origin has blessed you with beauty and scent. This blessing has led you to your death. For that, I am sorry, "But the Rose replied, "My purpose on earth is to show beauty to humanity to provide all with the fragrance of Love. I am a symbol of Love. That is why, I am offered by the lover to the Beloved. The prettier I am, and the more beautiful I smell, the stronger will be my message to humanity. So, do not be sorry for Me, for I have fulfilled My purpose – This should make you happy for both of us! You, too, are like a Rose to your Origin. So, when your mission is fulfilled, you too will be plucked from the garden to be with the Origin for Eternity. That is what life is all about." In a few hours, my dear Rose had wilted. That is the second message she had to give to me.

"We will all wilt one day. Death will come to us all. Complete your mission, and seek Union with the Origin before you wilt. For then, you will remain eternally fresh from within. Around you there are many reminders and signs. Do not be blind to them!" Then came her third and final message. "By the way, did you notice my thorns?

"This tells you that Life and Love can be beautiful but not always easy. There are thorns that will hurt you as they have hurt the greatest of people that have come before you. The Origin is your Healer. Become One with the Origin and each thorn will become to you a Rose in itself. Farewell my dear. I have delivered to you the three messages that I was sent to you for."

Amyn Dahya

REFLECTIONS from the ORIGIN

Be and It Is Volume 1

www.Mpowerment.co.uk

"You will either step forward into GROWTH, or you will step back into SAFETY. "

Abraham Maslow

DANGER
is REAL

FEAR is
a CHOICE!

Will Smith
From the movie, After Earth

To blow and swallow at the same moment is not easy.

NEITHER IS THINKING NEGATIVE WHILE YOU THINK POSITIVE OR FROWNING WHILE YOU SMILE.

www.Mpowerment.co.uk

Count Your Blessings

Learn to count the blessings that you have for they are truly yours
And don't grieve for what you do not have for it was never yours.
Appreciate what you have...

Amyn Dahya

The Law of Rhythm

The tide goes out...

night follows day ...

good times follows bad times...

order follows disorder.

When you are on a down swing,

do not feel bad.

Know the swing,

will changed and things will get better.

It's just the way life is,

so no matter what you're going through right now...

There are good times coming, think of them.

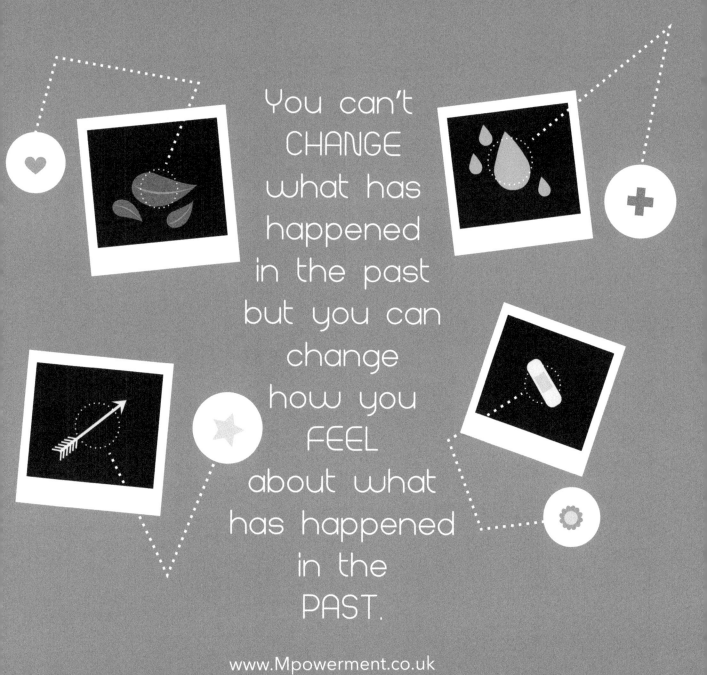

You can't CHANGE what has happened in the past but you can change how you FEEL about what has happened in the PAST.

www.Mpowerment.co.uk

It's Up To Me

i get discouraged now and then, when there are clouds of gray,
until i think about the things that happened yesterday. i do not mean the
day before or those of months ago, but all the yesterday in which i had
the chance to grow. i think of opportunities that i allowed to die, and
those i took advantage of before they passed me by. and i remember that
the past presented quite a plight, but somehow i endured it and the future
seemed all right. and i remind myself that i am capable and free,
and my success and happiness are really up to me.

James J. Metcalfe

" <u>(Insert your full name here)</u>, **You are a child of God and the being God made was never intended for the sort of weak, negative life you are leading. God made you for success not failure. God never made anyone to be a failure. You are perverting the great object of your existence by giving way to these miserable doubts of yourself, of your ability to be what you desire with all your heart to be. You should be ashamed to go out amongst your associates with a long, sad, dejected face, as though you were a misfit, as though you did not have the ability to do what your creator sent you here to do. You were made to express what you long to express. Why not do, this? Why not stand and walk like a conqueror, like a David who slew Goliath, instead of giving way to discouragement and doubt and carrying on like a failure? The image of Perfection, the image of your Creator lies within you. You must bring it to the center of your conscious thought and express it to the world. Don't disgrace your maker by violating that image, by being everything but the magnificent success God intended you to be. "**

BOB PROCTOR

PRESENCE

On a scale of (0-10), what level are you in this present moment in terms of your emotional, mental and physical vibrancy and presence?

What needs to change in order for you to be truly present with every single person (your partner, wife, children, work colleagues, team members, clients, customers etc.) you interact with today?

Information is a meal that is
received with gratitude,
savoured with joy,
digested in time
and returned once again
to the soil it came from.

Share information...

Amyn Dahya
Be and It Is Volume 1

MONEY
can buy everything

DREAMS

Love

TIME

Friends

happiness

except the things

we WANT and NEED the most!

~ G.L. Robertson ~

www.Mpowerment.co.uk

God doesn't
look at how much
we DO,

but with
how much
LOVE we do it.

Mother Teresa

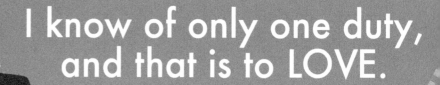

I know of only one duty,
and that is to LOVE.

Albert Camus

(1913-1960).ss

The Law of Cause and Effect

Whatever you send into the Universe comes back.
Action and re-action are equal and opposite.

So, say good things, to everyone, treat everyone with
total respect and it will all come back to you.
Never worry about what you are going to get,
just concentrate on what you can give and give it
with all your might and ability.

"Questions Are The Answer"
The Morning Power Questions

1. What am I happy about in my life right now?

What about that makes me happy? How does that make me feel?

2. What am I excited about in my life right now?

What about that makes me excited? How does that make me feel?

3. What am I proud about in my life right now?

What about that makes me proud? How does that make me feel?

4. What am I grateful about in my life right now?

What about that makes me grateful? How does that make me feel?

5. What am I enjoying most in my life right now?

What about that do I enjoy? How does that make me feel?

6. What am I committed to in my life right now?

What about that makes me committed? How does that make me feel?

7. Who do I love? Who loves me?

What about that makes me loving? How does that make me feel?

The Evening Power Questions

In the evening, ask the Morning Questions,
and then ask these additional questions:

1.What have I given today?

In what ways have I been a giver today?

2.What did I learn today?

3.How has today added to the quality of my life

(from Anthony Robbins, Awaken The Giant Within, Chapter 8 (pg. 204)

The Power of Habit

You may know me. I'm your constant companion.
I'm your greatest helper; I'm your heaviest burden.
I will push you onward or drag you down to failure.
I am at your command.
Half the tasks you do might as well be turned over to me.
I'm able to do them quickly, and I'm able to do them the
same way every time if that's what you want.
I'm easily managed; all you've got to do is to be firm with me.
Show me exactly how you want it done. I'll do it automatically.
I am the servant of all great men and women; of course,
servant of failures as well. I've made great individuals
who have ever been great. And I've made all the failures, too.
But I work with all the precision of a marvellous computer with
the intelligence of a human being.
You may run me for profit, or you may run me to ruin;
it makes no difference to me.
Take me. Be easy with me and I will destroy you.
Be firm with me and I'll put the world at your feet.
Who am I? I'm Habit!

Unknown

"REPETITION
IS THE MOTHER OF SKILL.

THAT WHICH SEEMS AND FEELS ARTIFICIAL AND CONTRIVED IN THE BEGINNING WILL SOON BECOME NATURAL AND NORMAL."

JOSEPH MCCLENDON III

www.Mpowerment.co.uk

The House of 1000 Mirrors

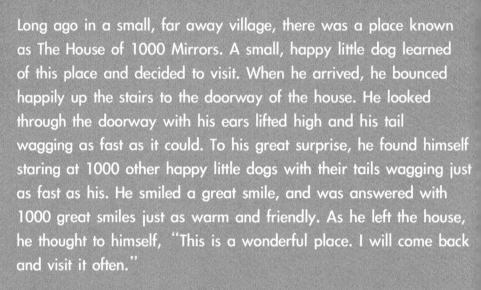

Long ago in a small, far away village, there was a place known as The House of 1000 Mirrors. A small, happy little dog learned of this place and decided to visit. When he arrived, he bounced happily up the stairs to the doorway of the house. He looked through the doorway with his ears lifted high and his tail wagging as fast as it could. To his great surprise, he found himself staring at 1000 other happy little dogs with their tails wagging just as fast as his. He smiled a great smile, and was answered with 1000 great smiles just as warm and friendly. As he left the house, he thought to himself, "This is a wonderful place. I will come back and visit it often."

In this same village, another little dog, who was not quite as happy as the first one, decided to visit the house. He slowly climbed the stairs and hung his head low as he looked into the door. When he saw 1000 unfriendly looking dogs staring back at him, he growled at them and was horrified to see 1000 little dogs growling back at him. As he left, he thought to himself, "That's a horrible place, and I will never go back there again"

All the faces in the world are mirrors

What kind of reflections do you see in the faces of people you meet?

Chinese Proverb

The Law of the Eternal Pool

The Eternal Pool provides all the resources of life,
from health to wealth, to wisdom and more.
Its law is simple to follow for that which comes
must also go to maintain its blessed flow.
Generosity is a two-way street.
For resources only flow through open hands,
one that gives, and one, that receives.
Discover abundance through giving...

Amyn Dahya
Be and It Is, Volume I

DETERMINE
WHO YOU ARE
AND WHAT YOU WANT
TO BECOME
BEFORE YOU DECIDE
WHAT YOU WANT
TO BE,
DO AND HAVE.

Who are you?

www.Mpowerment.co.uk

We think sometimes that poverty is only being hungry, naked and homeless.

The poverty of being unwanted, unloved and uncared for is the greatest poverty.

We must start in our own homes to remedy this kind of poverty.

Mother Teresa

"Our **deepest fear** is not that we are inadequate.

Our deepest fear is that we are **powerful beyond measure**.

It is our **light**, not our darkness that **most frightens us**.

We ask ourselves, 'Who am I to be brilliant, gorgeous, talented, fabulous?'

Actually, **who are you not to be?** You are a child of God.

Your playing small does not serve the world.

There is nothing enlightened about shrinking so that other people won't feel insecure around you.

We are all meant to shine, as children do.

We were born to make manifest the glory of God that is within us.

It's not just in some of us; it's in everyone.

And as we **let our own light shine,**

we unconsciously give other **people** permission to **do the same.**

As we are **liberated from our own fear,**

our presence automatically **liberates others.**"

∿MARIANNE WILLIAMSON ∿

The Law of Gender

every seed has
a gestation or
incubation period.

ideas are spiritual seeds
and will move into form
or physical results.

your goals will
manifest when
the time is right.

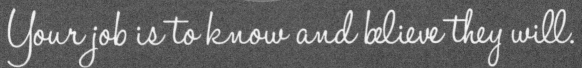

Your job is to know and believe they will.

www.Mpowerment.co.uk

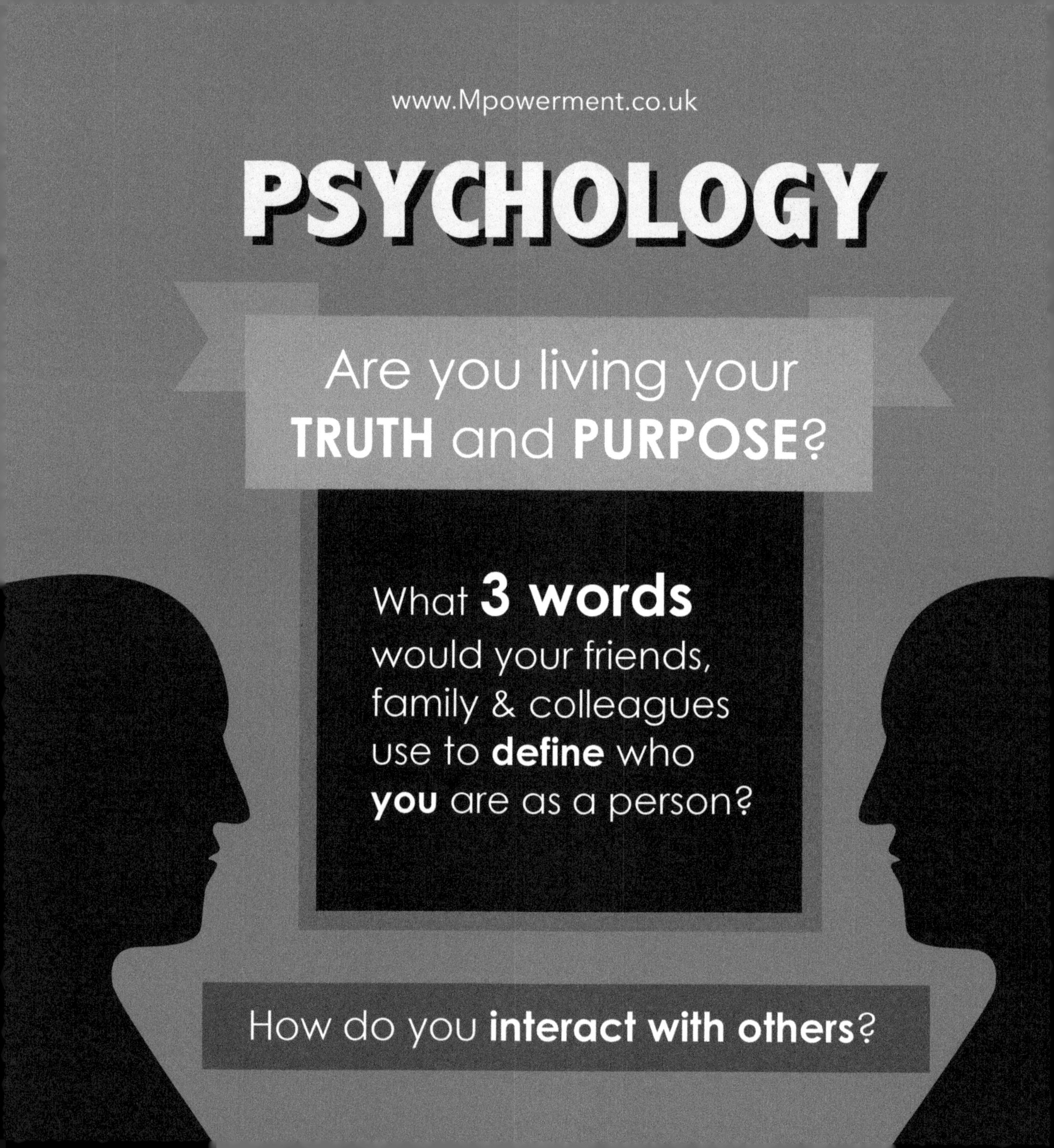

www.Mpowerment.co.uk
PSYCHOLOGY
Are you living your TRUTH and PURPOSE?
What 3 words would your friends, family & colleagues use to define who you are as a person?
How do you interact with others?

"Any IDEA that is held in the MIND,
that is EMPHASIZED, that is FEARED
or REVERED will begin AT ONCE

to cloth itself
in the most
convenient

and appropriate
form that is
available. "

Andrew Carnegie
as given to Napoleon Hill

www.Mpowerment.co.uk

"Faith in action is love,

and love in action is service.

By transforming that faith

into living acts of love,

you put yourself into contact

with your creator himself."

you are in total bliss

(in the zone).

DEATH

**Death is a continuation
of that which was interrupted by birth.**

**Life in this world is but a short stop
in the passage of eternity.**

Celebrate, life,
do not grieve...

Amyn Dahya
Be and it Is, Volme I

www.Mpowerment.co.uk

ALL is WELL

I am the wind. I am the rain. I am the sunlight through your windowpane, I am the leaf turning brown in the fall, I'm the faintest whisper on the breeze when you call, I am the snowflake that kisses your cheek, I'm the child In the park playing go hide and seek, I am the laughter that fills the spring air, I'm all around you I'm everywhere, I'll always be with you from this moment on. In your, every dance in your every song. You see when we move on we never truly die. We become one with nature. We unify. Take care my precious ones on my passing don't dwell, remember the love we shared together. See you again someday. All is well.

Andy Harrington

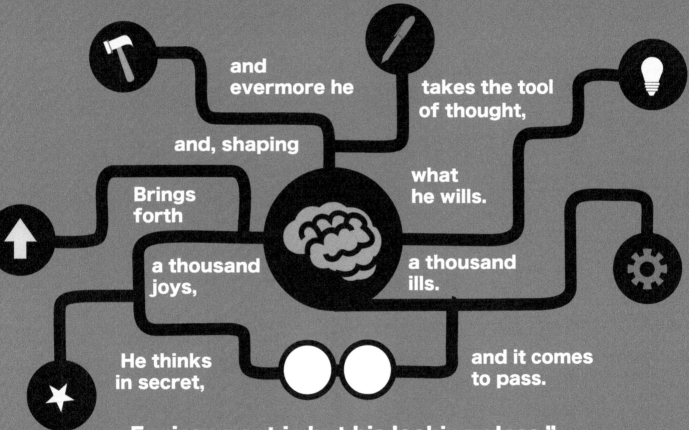

"MIND is the master power
that molds and makes and man is mind,

and
evermore he

takes the tool
of thought,

and, shaping

Brings
forth

what
he wills.

a thousand
joys,

a thousand
ills.

He thinks
in secret,

and it comes
to pass.

Environment is but his looking glass."

www.Mpowerment.co.uk **James Allen**

The Dreamers Are The Builders

" Dream lofty dreams, and as you dream, so you shall become.
Your VISION is the promise of what you shall one day BE;
your, IDEAL, is the prophecy of what you shall at last UNVEIL.
The greatest achievement was at first, and for a time, a dream.
The oak sleeps in the acorn; the bird waits in the egg;
and in the highest vision of the soul, a waking angel stirs.
Dreams are the seedlings of realities. Your circumstance may be
uncongenial, but they shall not long remain so, if you but perceive
an ideal and strive to reach it. You cannot travel WITHIN,
and stand still WITHOUT. "

James Allen

ORDER OF VISUALIZATION

"The exercise of the visualizing faculty keeps your mind in order, and attracts to you the things you need to make life more enjoyable, in an orderly way. If you train yourself in the practice of deliberately picturing your desire and carefully examining your picture, you will soon find that your thoughts and desires proceed in a more orderly procession than ever before. Having reached a state of ordered mentality, you are no longer in a constant state of mental hurry. 'Hurry' is 'Fear', and consequently destructive.

In other words, when your understanding grasps the power to visualize your heart's desire and hold it with your will, it attracts to you all things requisite to the fulfillment of that picture, by the harmonious vibrations of the law of attraction. You realize that since Order is Heaven's first law, and visualization places things in their natural order, then it must be a heavenly thing to visualize. Everyone visualizes, whether, they know it or not. Visualizing is the great secret of success. The conscious use of this great power attracts to you multiplied resources, intensifies your wisdom, and enables you to make use of advantages which you formerly failed to recognize."

GENEVIEVE BEHREND (YOUR INVISIBLE POWER)

For further copies of the,

" eMpower Yourself with 7 Natural Laws ",

visit and contact us at:

••

www.Mpowerment.co.uk

••

CPSIA information can be obtained
at www.ICGtesting.com
Printed in the USA
LVOW05*1416091115

461711LV00037B/423/P